COVER BY ROBB MOMMAERTS

With Special Thanks to Marisa Marionakis, Rick Blanco, Nicole Rivera, Conrad Montgomery, Meghan Bradley, Curtis Lelash, Kelly Crews and the wonderful folks at Cartoon Network.

ISSUE #1 COVER
BOB FLYNN

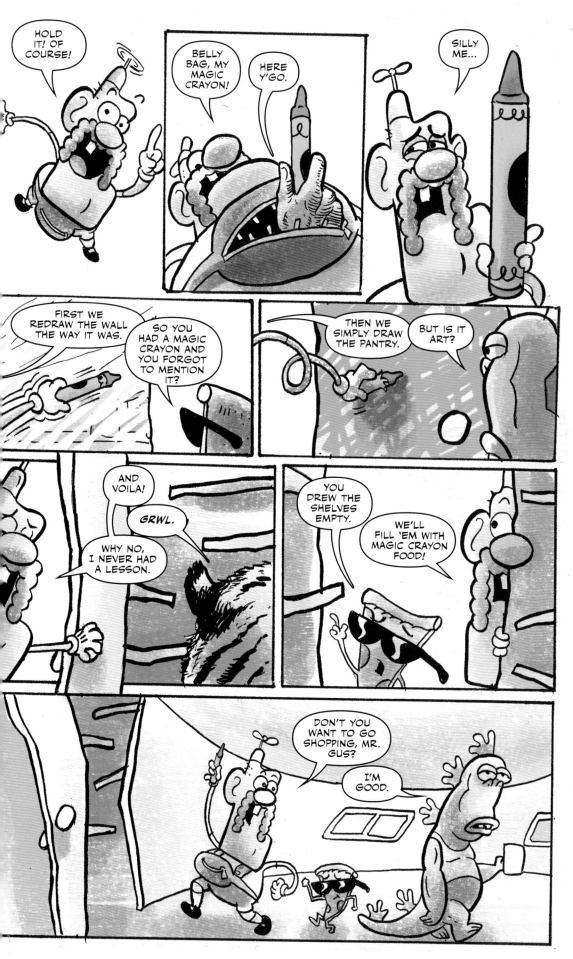

THE SCARIEST STORY EVER
BY JIMMY GIEGERICH

AND WHEN THE CREAKY DOOR FINALLY OPENED, THE CREEPY OLD MAN SAID...

"YO, I'M A GHOST."

AHHH!

THAT WAS SO SCARY I DIED...

OF BOREDOM!

OH YEAH?! THINK YOU CAN DO BETTER?

NO PROBLEMO, BROSEF!

THIS STORY IS CALLED...

THE SCARIEST STORY YOU'LL HEAR IN YOUR LIFE EVER IN HISTORY!

ONCE UPON A TIME, IN THE CREEPIEST FOREST EVER

THERE WAS A MONSTER UNLIKE ANY MONSTER YOU'VE SEEN!

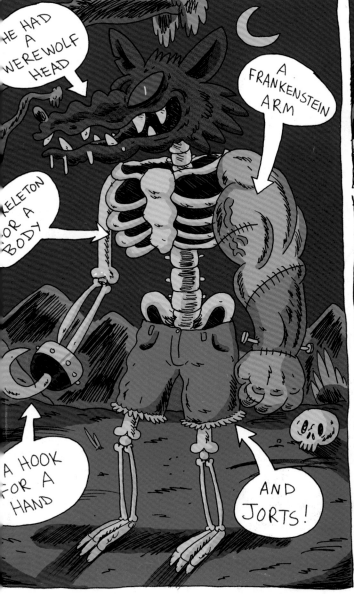

HE HAD A WEREWOLF HEAD

A FRANKENSTEIN ARM

KELETON OR A BODY

A HOOK OR A HAND

AND JORTS!

ON NIGHTS LIKE TONIGHT, HE'D WAIT FOR PEOPLE LEAVING BURGER HUT...

AND ATTACK THEM!

AND EAT THEIR BURGERS & FRIES ALIVE!

SOMETIMES YOU CAN HEAR THEIR CRIES FROM THOSE WOODS AT NIGHT...

LEGEND HAS IT...

HE'S ON HIS WAY TO THIS SLEEPOVER.

RAHH!!

SUP, UNCLE G?

SLAP!

HEY BUDDY!

THE END

FEAR OF WATER

EVGENY YAKOVLE

END

END

YEHUDI MERCADO

END.

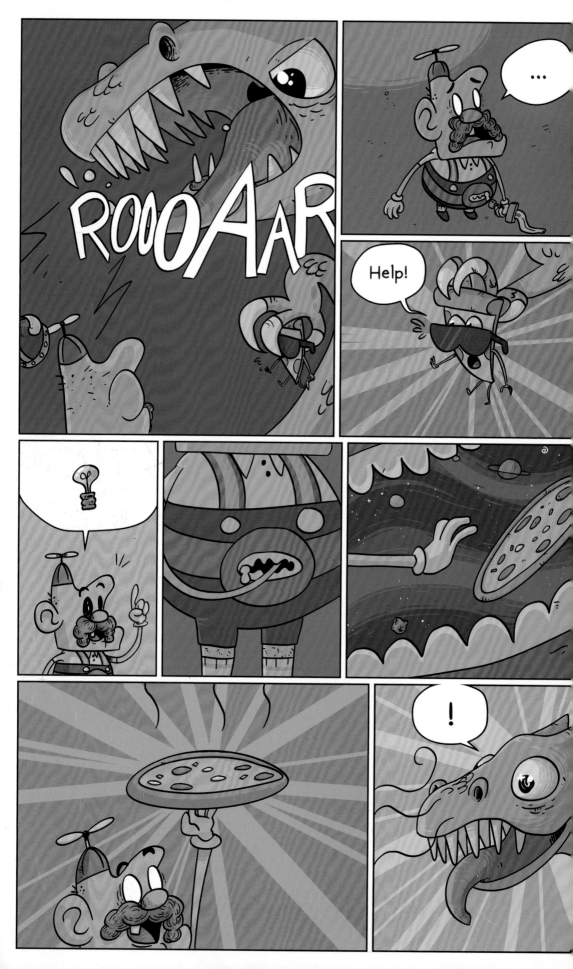

HEY KIDS!! DO THE PIZZA STEVE DANCE!

BY JIMMY GIEGERICH

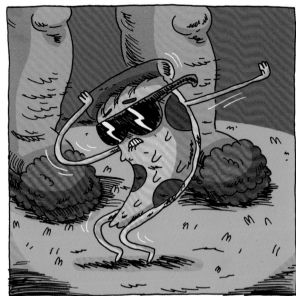

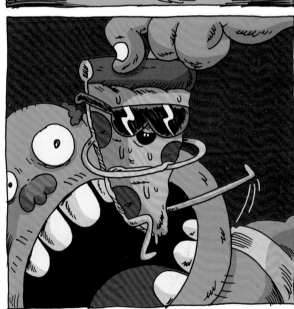

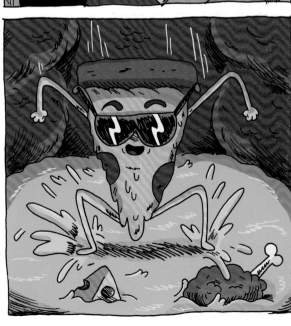

THE
END

"SCRATCH THAT"

WRITTEN & DRAWN BY LAURA HOWELL

END

YEHUDI MERCADO

Sorry, Uncle Grandpa, I don't feel so good.

We have to get you better!

C'mon Steve! Let's get Belly Bag better!

How we going to do that, Uncle G?

We're going to a place I never wanted to go to again...

...The Soup Dimension!

Oh, no! Not the Soup Dimension!

What's the big deal about the Soup Dimension?

Well, Pizza Steve, Many, Many, Uncles ago...

SWEET! A flashback!

END!

SOLVE THE PUZZLE TO FREE UNCLE GRANDPA

Pizza Doughnut Burger Game
Tiger Toys Fries Poster
Emperor Laser Radio Television
Candy Ghost Comic Rocket
Grandpa Steve Good Morning
Alien Marshmallow Library

```
N C N G A W H E V R L H T C C
A C L R E O J I M A E E Z I X
D G P A W L N B S P K G M W N
F A E N R L E E J C E O R O L
F M N D E A R F O G C R I U F
R E J P T M H R J T V S O T B
I X R A S H R M O D I C I R G
E A X O O S O Y Z V O I D A R
S T B K P R S W E P I Z Z A I
Y A Z W N A U L Y R A R B I L
T D L I V M E D O U G H N U T
A I N I S T E V E L L Y S P S
M G G A E D O O G P S T R E O
Q J T E C N N I K W T D W A H
T V V F R J N J B Q S F P E G
```

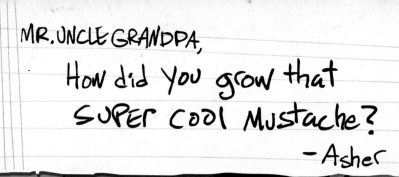

MR. UNCLE GRANDPA,
How did you grow that
SUPER COOL Mustache?

—Asher

"YOU START BY KNEADING THE DOUGH WITH GENTLE FINGERS.

"ROLL THE DOUGH WITH THE THICKNESS OF A COZY BLANKET.

"PLACE INTO A WOOD FIRED OVEN FOR THE LENGTH OF A SECRET.

"WHILE IT BAKES, TAKE A LITTLE TIME FOR YOURSELF.

"IMMEDIATELY TAKE IT OUT OF THE OVEN AND THROW IT ON YOUR FACE!"

OWWWWW

ISSUE #2 VARIANT COVER
NICK EDWARDS

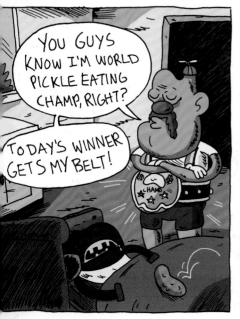

A Tangle of Torso Dangles

BY **NICHOL ASHWORTH**
COLORS BY **WHITNEY COGAR**

UNCLE GRANDPA HAS, LIKE, A BAJILLION ARMS AND THEY'RE ALL TANGLED UP! GO THROUGH THE MAZE AND FIGURE OUT WHICH HAND AND ARM ARE ATTACHED TO THE CLEFT IN HIS CHIN!

The correct answer is: the hand with the globe.

UNCLE GRANDPA'S DREAMLAND

UNCLE GRANDPA HAS FALLEN INTO A DEEP SLEEP. THIS IS HIS DREAMLAND, WHERE EVERYBODY AND EVERYTHING LOOKS LIKE UNCLE GRANDPA TOO. THE REAL UNCLE GRANDPA IS STILL FAST ASLEEP. HELP US FIND HIM AND WAKE HIM UP! ALONG WITH UNCLE GRANDPA, WE ALSO NEED TO FIND MR. GUS, PIZZA STEVE, BELLY BAG, AND GIANT REALISTIC FLYING TIGER.

HERE ARE SOME OTHER OBJECTS YOU CAN FIND IN THE DREAMSCAPE TOO:

FUEL

UNCLE GRANDPA GETS THE SPINS! BY KEVIN BURKHALTER

END!

AND THAT'S WHY I LET *MY* NOSE PICK ME!

AND... WE'RE OUT! COMIC BOOK IS BACK IN :30.

THE CUE CARD GUY WAS LATE ON THE KNOCK KNOCK JOKE.

DON'T WORRY ABOUT IT, UNCLE G. HE'LL BE GONE BY THE LAST PANEL.

AND THE LIGHTING GUY IS GIVING ME A SUNBURN.

HE'S HISTORY.

JUST CONCENTRATE ON BEING THE STAR, UNCLE G. THERE'S NOBODY ELSE LIKE YOU, BABE.

BY YEHUDI MERCADO

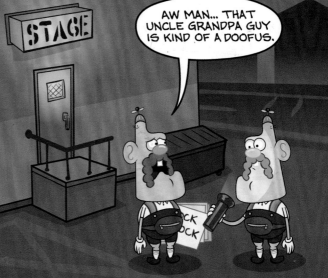

AW MAN... THAT UNCLE GRANDPA GUY IS KIND OF A DOOFUS.

STAGE

END.

IT'S NOT A STORY, IT'S...

THE LEGENDARY LEGENDS OF PIZZA STEVE

ROAD RAGE
by Yehudi Mercado

END.

UNCLE GRANDPA IN "FROWN TOWN"

BY DAVID DEGRAND

BY YEHUDI MERCADO

END.

ISSUE #3 VARIANT COVER
BRANDON REESE

END

Ballroom Dancing Search-and-Find

by Nichol Ashworth

5 Uncle Grandpas ✓	6 Roses ✓	2 Ice-skating Rinks ✓
2 Tutus ✓	1 Dimensional Rift ✓	2 Christmas Trees ✓
3 Pairs of Dancers ✓	1 Theft in-progress ✓	1 Cake ✓
7 Gifts ✓	2 Top Hats ✓	1 Unicorn ✓

CHRISTINE LARSEN 2014

UHNN...

WHERE AM I?

THIS PLACE IS WEIRD.

I KNEW ALL THIS WEIRDNESS WOULD GET ME ONE DAY.

UNCLE GRANDPA! WHERE ARE YOU?

UNCLE GRAND-

RUSTLE!

-PA?

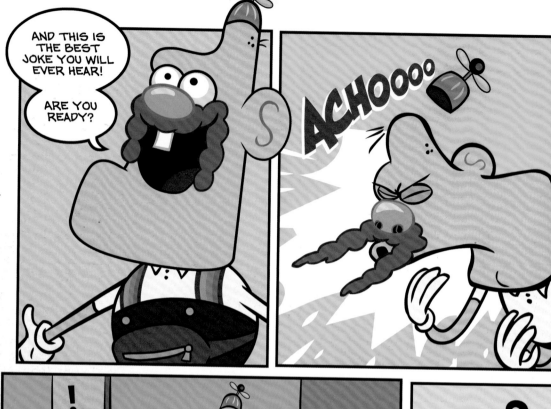

BY YEHUDI MERCADO

END.

LEMONMOO

EVGENY YAKOVLEV

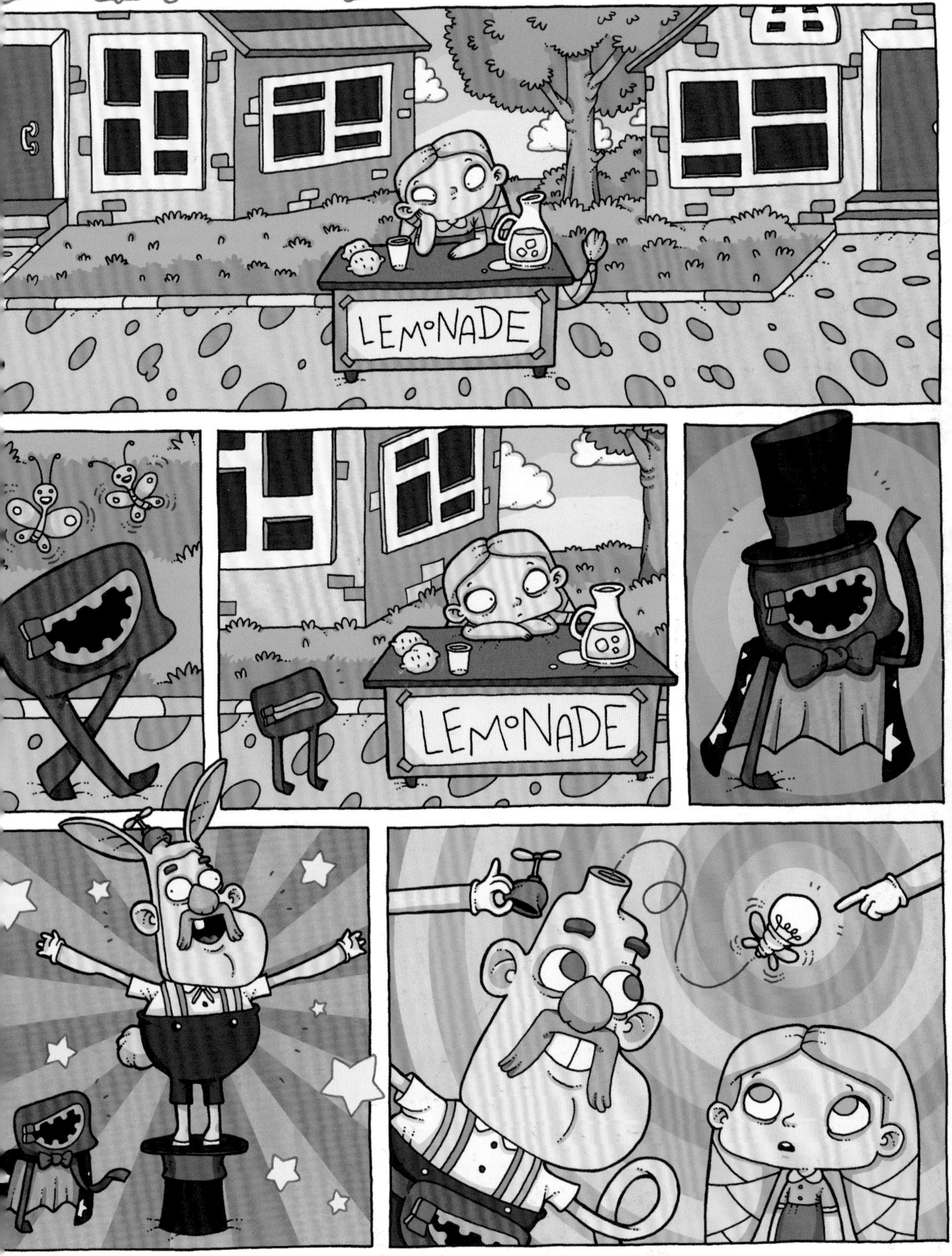

END

UNCLE GRANDPA IN "A SLICE OF HORROR"

BY DAV DEG

END

ISSUE #1 BOOM! STUDIOS EXCLUSIVE COV
TRAVIS H
WITH COLORS BY WHITNEY COG

ISSUE #2 COVER
GENY YAKOVLEV

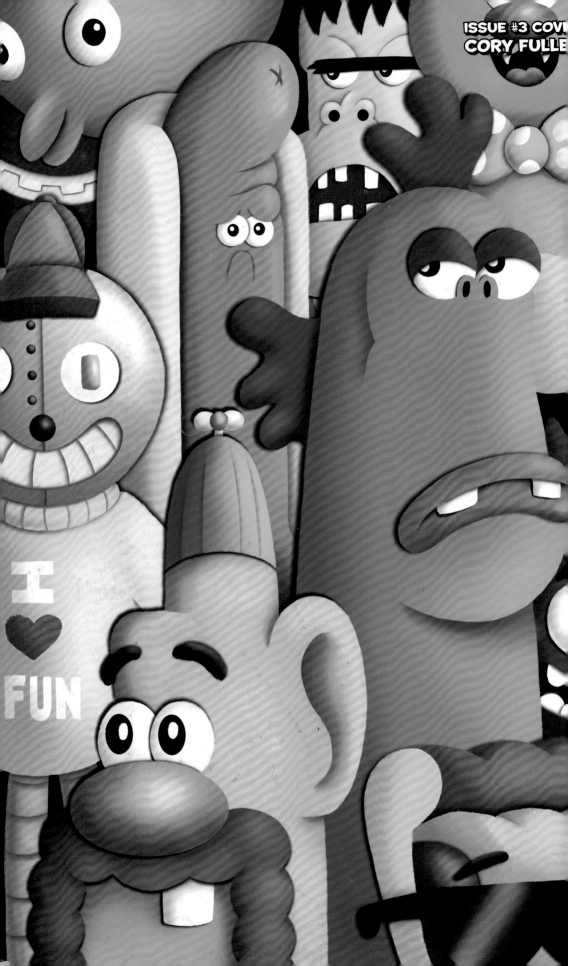

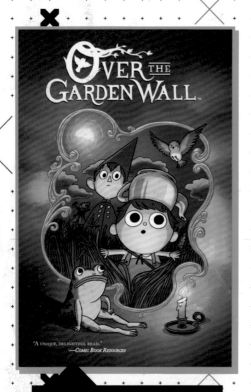

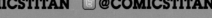

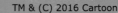

**CLARENCE
VOLUME 1
On Sale: December**

Chicken Phantom

**CLARENCE OGN:
CHICKEN PHANTOM
On Sale: January**

**UNCLE GRANDPA &
THE TIME CASSEROLE
On Sale: February**

**AMAZING WORLD OF
GUMBALL VOLUME 1
On Sale: March**